Which Bible is Better?

How to Compare Various
Versions of the Bible

Fr. Joseph Gleason

Which Bible is Better?
How to Compare Various Versions of the Bible
by Fr. Joseph Gleason

Copyright © 2014 by Fr. Joseph M. Gleason

Printed in the United States of America. All rights in this book are reserved. No part of the book may be used or reproduced without written permission except in the case of brief quotations embodied in articles and books.

Publisher's Cataloging-in-Publication

Gleason, Joseph M., 1978-

    Which Bible is Better?: How to compare various versions of the Bible / by Joseph M. Gleason:—1st ed. 60 p.

    ISBN 978-1-312-50555-1

    1. Bible Versions 2. Eastern Orthodoxy 3. Septuagint 4. Masoretic Text

Scripture quotations marked (NIV) are taken from the Holy Bible, New International Version®, NIV®. Copyright © 1973, 1978, 1984, 2011 by Biblica, Inc.™ Used by permission of Zondervan. All rights reserved worldwide. www.zondervan.com The "NIV" and "New International Version" are trademarks registered in the United States Patent and Trademark Office by Biblica, Inc.™

Old Testament Scripture quotations marked (OSB) are taken from the St. Athanasius Academy Septuagint.™ Copyright © 2008 by St. Athanasius Academy of Orthodox Theology. Used by permission. All rights reserved.

New Testament Scripture quotations marked (OSB) are taken from the New King James Version®. Copyright © 1982 by Thomas Nelson, Inc. Used by permission. All rights reserved.

www.omahaorthodox.com

Table of Contents

5 – With So Many Bibles, How Do We Choose?

7 – Psalm 14 – According to the Apostle Paul

9 – Psalm 4 – According to the Apostle Paul

9 – Psalm 40 – According to the Book of Hebrews

11 – Genesis 46 – According to Stephen

11 – Isaiah 53 – According to the Apostle Peter

12 – Isaiah 10 – According to the Apostle Paul

15 – Isaiah 61 – According to Jesus *(Did Jesus Tell a Lie?)*

23 – Who was Job?

27 – Where is God in the Book of Esther?

33 – Evicting Martyrs from the Hall of Faith

37 – Erasing a Prophecy of Christ

45 – Where Did All These Differences Come From?

59 – Which Bible is Better?

With So Many Bibles, How Do We Choose?

A lot has changed since the middle ages. At that time, Bibles were copied by hand, and only the very rich could afford to own one. If you were familiar with Scripture, it was because you listened carefully in church. And if you wanted to read a Bible, you would probably have to go to a church or monastery. But today, you can walk into a Christian bookstore and be inundated with literally hundreds of different choices . . .

Different Bible Versions:

King James Version (KJV)
New International Version (NIV)
Revised Standard Version (RSV)
American Standard Version (ASV)
Complete Jewish Bible (CJB)
Douay-Rheims 1899 (DRA)
English Standard Version (ESV)
Orthodox Study Bible (OSB)
New English Translation (NET)
New American Standard (NASB)
Young's Literal Translation (YLT)
Amplified Bible
The Message
and many more . . .

Bibles with Different Study Notes:

Oxford Study Bible
New Interpreters Study Bible
Geneva Study Bible
Women's Study Bible
Men's Study Bible
Life Application Study Bible
Orthodox Study Bible
Ryrie Study Bible
Joyce Meyer Study Bible
Reformation Study Bible
Dake Annotated Reference Bible
and many more . . .

With all of these choices, how can the average reader find the best Bible for personal study? Is it just a matter of personal preference, or does it matter?

Not all Bibles are created equal:

- Some Bibles are easy to read. *Some are more difficult.*
- Some Bibles have study notes. *Some have the text of Scripture alone.*
- Some Bibles have 75 books. Some have 73 books. *Some have 66 books.*
- Some Bibles are accurate translations. *Some are not so accurate.*

In this book, we will compare three popular versions of the Bible:

- King James Version (KJV)
- New International Version (NIV)
- Orthodox Study Bible (OSB)

There are many other translations we could examine, but by looking at these three versions, we will encounter many of the significant differences which render a Bible either accurate or inaccurate. In every case, please feel free to look up the same passages in any version of the Bible that you prefer. Compare your Bible with the Bibles referenced in this book, and see how well it stands the test.

Throughout this book, we will frequently use the New Testament as a guide, to help identify the most accurate translations of Scripture. When Jesus and the apostles quote from other books of the Bible, we believe their quotations are correct. If Jesus quotes from Scripture, we look for the Bible which most closely matches the quotation Jesus himself provided. If the apostle Paul quotes from Scripture, we favor the Bible which most accurately matches his quotation. The strategy is simple: *"If it is good enough for Jesus and the apostles, it is good enough for us!"*

Psalm 14 - According to the Apostle Paul

To begin, we can compare Psalm 14 in various versions of the Bible, and then see how St. Paul quotes from that Psalm in the New Testament. (If you have a Bible that is translated from the Septuagint, it will be numbered as Psalm 13.)

St. Paul had a thorough understanding of the Old Testament scriptures, and he frequently quoted from them, revealing the truth of Christ's message. In the book of Romans, before demonstrating that Jesus is our savior, Paul first demonstrates the depths of our sin, so that we know what we need to be saved *from*. He quotes from this Psalm, showing that human sin has been a problem for a very long time.

In the three columns below, we will compare this Psalm in the King James Version (KJV), the New International Version (NIV), and the Orthodox Study Bible (OSB). If you have another version of the Bible, feel free to open it to Psalm 14, and compare it with what you see here:

King James	**NIV**	**Orthodox Study Bible**
They are all gone aside, they are all together become filthy: there is none that doeth good, no, not one. (Psalm 14:3)	All have turned away, all have become corrupt; there is no one who does good, not even one. (Psalm 14:3)	All turned aside and were altogether corrupted; There was not even one doing good, no, not one. Their throat is an open tomb; They deal deceptively with their tongues; The poison of serpents is under their lips, Whose mouth is full of curses and bitterness; Their feet are swift to shed blood; Affliction and suffering are in their ways, And the way of peace they have not known; There is no fear of God before their eyes. (Psalm 13:3)

It is easy to see that these Bibles are very different from each other. The KJV and NIV readings are very short, while the OSB reading is considerably longer. But which one is correct? Have the KJV and NIV taken away from the Word of God, or has the OSB added to it?

To answer this question, we can turn to the New Testament, and ask the Apostle Paul. In the third chapter of the book of Romans, St. Paul quotes from this Psalm:

King James	**NIV**	**Orthodox Study Bible**
As it is written, There is none righteous, no, not one: There is none that understandeth, there is none that seeketh after God. They are all gone out of the way, they are together become unprofitable; there is none that doeth good, no, not one. Their throat is an open sepulchre; with their tongues they have used deceit; the poison of asps is under their lips: Whose mouth is full of cursing and bitterness: Their feet are swift to shed blood: Destruction and misery are in their ways: And the way of peace have they not known: There is no fear of God before their eyes.	As it is written: There is no one righteous, not even one; there is no one who understands; there is no one who seeks God. All have turned away, they have together become worthless; there is no one who does good, not even one. Their throats are open graves; their tongues practice deceit. The poison of vipers is on their lips. Their mouths are full of cursing and bitterness. Their feet are swift to shed blood; ruin and misery mark their ways, and the way of peace they do not know. There is no fear of God before their eyes.	As it is written: There is none righteous, no, not one; There is none who understands; There is none who seeks after God. They have all turned aside; They have together become unprofitable; There is none who does good, no, not one. Their throat is an open tomb; With their tongues they have practiced deceit; The poison of asps is under their lips; Whose mouth is full of cursing and bitterness. Their feet are swift to shed blood; Destruction and misery are in their ways; And the way of peace they have not known. There is no fear of God before their eyes.
(Romans 3:10-18)	(Romans 3:10-18)	(Romans 3:10-18)

In Romans 3:10, St. Paul says, "It is written," indicating that he is quoting from Scripture. Then, in verses ten through eighteen, he gives an extended quote from the Psalms.

Yet, in the KJV, this entire passage is not anywhere in the Psalms. Was the Apostle Paul lying? Likewise, in the NIV, this entire passage cannot be found in the Psalms. Was he misquoting Scripture?

Of course, St. Paul was telling the truth. He was not misquoting Scripture. If he wrote the book of Romans, and if he said, "As it is written," then we can rest assured he is providing an accurate quote from the Old Testament.

But if the Apostle Paul was accurate in the book of Romans, that means both the KJV and the NIV have inaccurate copies of Psalm 14. Those versions of the Bible have taken away from the Word of God. Unanimously, every version of the New Testament agrees that the Orthodox Study Bible contains the correct Psalm reading.

Psalm 4 – According to the Apostle Paul

Now let's take a look at Psalm 4:4 in various versions of the Bible. (If you have a Bible that is translated from the Septuagint, it will be numbered as Psalm 4:5.)

King James	NIV	Orthodox Study Bible
Stand in awe, and sin not: commune with your own heart upon your bed, and be still. Selah.	Tremble and do not sin; when you are on your beds, search your hearts and be silent.	**Be angry, and do not sin;** Have remorse upon your beds For what you say in your hearts.
(Psalm 4:4)	(Psalm 4:4)	(Psalm 4:5)

In the New Testament, the Apostle Paul quotes from this Psalm, reminding us to avoid sinning whenever we become angry:

King James	NIV	Orthodox Study Bible
Be ye angry, and sin not: let not the sun go down upon your wrath	**"In your anger do not sin":** Do not let the sun go down while you are still angry	**"Be angry, and do not sin":** do not let the sun go down on your wrath
(Ephesians 4:26)	(Ephesians 4:26)	(Ephesians 4:26)

Which version of the Psalms was St. Paul using? Unanimously, every version of the New Testament agrees that the Orthodox Study Bible provides the correct Psalm reading.

Psalm 40 – According to the Book of Hebrews

Now we can compare Psalm 40 in various versions of the Bible. (If you have a Bible that is translated from the Septuagint, it will be numbered as Psalm 39.)

King James	NIV	Orthodox Study Bible
Sacrifice and offering thou didst not desire; mine ears hast thou opened: burnt offering and sin offering hast thou not required.	Sacrifice and offering you did not desire — but my ears you have opened — burnt offerings and sin offerings you did not require.	Sacrifice and offering You did not will; But **a body You prepared for me;** A whole burnt offering and a sin offering You did not require.
(Psalm 40:6)	(Psalm 40:6)	(Psalm 39:7)

These verses are very different from each other. The KJV and NIV readings say, "my ears you have opened," while the OSB says, "a body You prepared for me." But which one is correct? Clearly, these translations are so different from one another, they cannot all be correct. Have the KJV and NIV correctly preserved the Word of God, or did the OSB get it right?

To answer this question, we can turn to the New Testament, and ask the author of the book of Hebrews. In the tenth chapter of Hebrews, he quotes from this Psalm. According to him, does this Psalm say "a body you have prepared for me," or "my ears you have opened"?

King James	**NIV**	**Orthodox Study Bible**
Wherefore when he cometh into the world, he saith, Sacrifice and offering thou wouldest not, but **a body hast thou prepared me**: In burnt offerings and sacrifices for sin thou hast had no pleasure.	Therefore, when Christ came into the world, he said: "Sacrifice and offering you did not desire, but **a body you prepared for me**; with burnt offerings and sin offerings you were not pleased."	Therefore, when He came into the world, He said: "Sacrifice and offering You did not desire, But **a body You have prepared for Me**. In burnt offerings and sacrifices for sin You had no pleasure."
(Hebrews 10:5-6)	(Hebrews 10:5-6)	(Hebrews 10:5-6)

The author of Hebrews refers to the incarnation of Jesus Christ, when a human body was prepared for Him. As testimony to the incarnation, Hebrews 10:5-6 quotes from Scripture.

Yet, according to the King James Version, this passage of Scripture cannot be found anywhere in the Bible. Likewise, according to the New International Version, this verse is found nowhere in Scripture. Was the author of Hebrews lying to us? Was he misquoting Scripture? Is this reference to the incarnation supposed to be absent from the Psalms?

Of course not. He was not being dishonest, and we have no reason to believe that he was misquoting Scripture. If he wrote the book of Hebrews, and if he references a passage of Scripture, then we can rest assured that he is providing an accurate quote from the Old Testament.

But if the book of Hebrews is accurate, that means both the KJV and the NIV have inaccurate copies of Psalm 40. Those versions of the Bible have changed the Word of God.

Unanimously, every version of the New Testament agrees that the Orthodox Study Bible contains the correct Psalm reading.

Genesis 46 – According to Stephen

Now, let's compare Genesis 46 in various versions of the Bible. How many people from Jacob's family came into Egypt?

King James	NIV	Orthodox Study Bible
And the sons of Joseph, which were born him in Egypt, were two souls: all the souls of the house of Jacob, which came into Egypt, were **threescore and ten**.	With the two sons who had been born to Joseph in Egypt, the members of Jacob's family, which went to Egypt, were **seventy** in all.	The sons of Joseph born to him in the land of Egypt were nine. Thus all the souls of Jacob's house who went to Egypt were **seventy-five**.
(Genesis 46:27)	(Genesis 46:27)	(Genesis 46:27)

These verses give different answers from one another. The KJV and NIV say that 70 people came into Egypt, while the OSB says it was 75. According to Stephen, the one speaking in Acts chapter 7, which number is correct?

King James	NIV	Orthodox Study Bible
Then sent Joseph, and called his father Jacob to him, and all his kindred, **threescore and fifteen** souls.	After this, Joseph sent for his father Jacob and his whole family, **seventy-five** in all.	Then Joseph sent and called his father Jacob and all his relatives to him, **seventy-five** people.
(Acts 7:14)	(Acts 7:14)	(Acts 7:14)

Seventy-five people from Jacob's family came into Egypt. Unanimously, every version of the New Testament agrees that the Orthodox Study Bible is correct.

Isaiah 53 – According to the Apostle Peter

Let's take a look at Isaiah 53 in various versions of the Bible:

King James	NIV	Orthodox Study Bible
. . . he had done no violence, neither was any deceit in his mouth.	. . . he had done no violence, nor was any deceit in his mouth.	. . . He committed **no lawlessness**, nor was deceit found in His mouth.
(Isaiah 53:9)	(Isaiah 53:9)	(Isaiah 53:9)

These verses give different prophecies. The KJV and NIV readings say that the coming Messiah will be without violence, while the OSB says that He will be completely without sin. (The word "lawlessness" is a synonym for "sin".) According to the New Testament, which prophecy is more accurate?

King James	NIV	Orthodox Study Bible
For even hereunto were ye called: because Christ also suffered for us, leaving us an example, that ye should follow his steps: **Who did no sin, neither was guile found in his mouth** (1 Peter 2:21-22)	To this you were called, because Christ suffered for you, leaving you an example, that you should follow in his steps. **"He committed no sin, and no deceit was found in his mouth."** (1 Peter 2:21-22)	For to this you were called, because Christ also suffered for us, leaving us an example, that you should follow His steps: **"Who committed no sin, Nor was deceit found in His mouth"** (1 Peter 2:21-22)

In this passage of Scripture, the Apostle Peter quotes from the book of Isaiah, and says it was prophesied that Jesus would be entirely without sin. The KJV and the NIV both have inaccurate copies of the book of Isaiah, which do not match the quotation provided in the book of 1 Peter. But the OSB doesn't have this problem.

Unanimously, every version of the New Testament agrees that the Orthodox Study Bible contains an accurate account of Isaiah's prophecy.

Isaiah 10 – According to the Apostle Paul

Let's take a look at Isaiah 10 in various versions of the Bible. In the KJV and NIV, Isaiah says a remnant of Israel would return to their land. But nothing is said of their salvation. Meanwhile, the Orthodox Study Bible predicts salvation of the remnant:

King James	NIV	Orthodox Study Bible
For though thy people Israel be as the sand of the sea, yet a remnant of them shall return (Isaiah 10:22)	Though your people be like the sand by the sea, Israel, only a remnant will return. (Isaiah 10:22)	For though the people of Israel be as the sand of the sea, **a remnant of them shall be saved** (Isaiah 10:22)

Which version of Isaiah is correct? Did he only say that Israel would return to their land? Or did he prophesy that a remnant of Israel would be saved?

King James	**NIV**	**Orthodox Study Bible**
Esaias also crieth concerning Israel, Though the number of the children of Israel be as the sand of the sea, **a remnant shall be saved**	Isaiah cries out concerning Israel: "Though the number of the Israelites be like the sand by the sea, only **the remnant will be saved."**	Isaiah also cries out concerning Israel: "Though the number of the children of Israel be as the sand of the sea, **The remnant will be saved."**
(Romans 9:27)	(Romans 9:27)	(Romans 9:27)

Unanimously, every version of the New Testament agrees that the Orthodox Study Bible has the correct prophecy recorded in the book of Isaiah.

In Scripture so far, we have heard from St. Paul, St. Stephen, and St. Peter. In the next passage, we will consider the testimony of Jesus himself.

Did Jesus Tell A Lie?

If you were faced with a hundred different Bible teachers, you might become frustrated and confused, trying to figure out which teachers are trustworthy, and which teachers are just blind guides.

But suppose that these teachers all used different versions of the Bible. You begin to look at them carefully, and ninety-nine of these Bibles have verses in them which say, "Jesus is a liar." Only one Bible says that you can trust what Jesus says. Would that help you narrow down the playing field? Would you trust any teacher who uses a false Bible? Or would you rather put your trust in the one, solitary teacher who has an accurate copy of the Scriptures?

In Luke 4, Jesus talks about healing the blind, and He quotes from the 61st chapter of Isaiah. We know that Jesus is trustworthy. We can trust that He quoted Isaiah accurately.

But when we review various versions of the Bible, are they in agreement with what Jesus said? Or are there certain copies of Scripture which would make Jesus out to be a liar?

To investigate this question, we can begin with this prophecy from the prophet Isaiah:

> The Spirit of the Lord is upon Me,
> because of which He anointed Me.
> He sent Me to proclaim good news to the poor,
> to heal the brokenhearted, to preach liberty to the captives
> **and recovery of sight to the blind;**
> to declare the acceptable year of the Lord . . .
>
> (Isaiah 61:2 – Orthodox Study Bible)

In the fourth chapter of the Gospel of Luke,
Jesus reads a prophecy from Isaiah, and says it is a prophecy of Himself:

> Then Jesus returned in the power of the Spirit to Galilee, and news of Him went out through all the surrounding region. And He taught in their synagogues, being glorified by all.
>
> So He came to Nazareth, where He had been brought up. And as His custom was, He went into the synagogue on the Sabbath day, and stood up to read. And He was handed the book of the prophet Isaiah. And when He had opened the book, He found the place where it was written:

> "The Spirit of the LORD is upon Me,
> Because He has anointed Me To preach the gospel to the poor;
> He has sent Me to heal the brokenhearted,
> To proclaim liberty to the captives
> **And recovery of sight to the blind,**
> To set at liberty those who are oppressed;
> To proclaim the acceptable year of the LORD."
>
> Then He closed the book, and gave it back to the attendant and sat down. And the eyes of all who were in the synagogue were fixed on Him. And He began to say to them, "Today this Scripture is fulfilled in your hearing." (Luke 4:14-21)

Jesus quotes Isaiah's prophecy,
and **says** that He himself is the fulfillment of this prophecy.
Throughout the rest of the Gospel of Luke, whenever Jesus heals blind men,
He **demonstrates** that He is the fulfillment of this prophecy.

In the 7th chapter of Luke, John the Baptist sends two of his disciples to ask Jesus about His identity. They say, "Are You the Coming One, or do we look for another?" They weren't asking if Jesus is an amazing person. They were specifically asking whether Jesus is the Messiah, the fulfillment of the prophecies in Scripture.

In the same hour that they asked this question, Luke 7:21 says that Jesus "cured many of their infirmities and plagues, and of evil spirits; **and unto many that were blind he gave sight.**"

"Then Jesus answering said unto them, Go your way, and tell John what things ye have seen and heard; how that **the blind see**, the lame walk, the lepers are cleansed, the deaf hear, the dead are raised, to the poor the gospel is preached. And blessed is he, whosoever shall not be offended in me." (Luke 7:22-23)

Just like Jesus had done in the synagogue earlier in the book of Luke, Jesus again points back to Isaiah's prophecy, which said that the coming Messiah would preach the Gospel to the poor, and give recovery of sight to the blind. In response to the disciples of John the Baptist, Jesus refers to Isaiah's prophecy, and demonstrates the prophecy's fulfillment by healing blind men before their very eyes.

In the 18th chapter of Luke, as Jesus came near Jericho, there was a blind beggar by the side of the road, who cried out, "Jesus, Son of David, have mercy on me." (Luke 18:38). Jesus again heals the blind, demonstrating that He himself is the fulfillment of the Messianic prophecy in Isaiah.

In Luke 14, Jesus gives a parable of the kingdom of heaven, where the poor, the maimed, the lame, and the blind are invited to a great feast. Of course, their invitation to the kingdom of heaven implies their ultimate healing. Jesus doesn't invite the blind into his kingdom so that they can stay blind; He invites them into his kingdom so that they can receive their sight.

Jesus also discusses blindness in the 6th chapter of Luke. He says blindness is not only a physical problem, but also a spiritual problem. Just as physical blindness can make one fall into a ditch, spiritual blindness can make one fall into heresy:

"And He spoke a parable to them: 'Can the blind lead the blind? Will they not both fall into the ditch? A disciple is not above his teacher, but everyone who is perfectly trained will be like his teacher.'" (Luke 6:39-40)

Imagine you are blind.
Multiple people are competing to be your teachers.
How do you figure out which teachers are blind, and which teachers can see?

Get each teacher alone in a room, and try some simple tests:

- Hold up a certain number of fingers, and ask them how many.
- Get a booklet that you are already familiar with. Ask them to read it.

If you were blind, and a person failed simple tests like these, would you accept that person as your teacher? Of course not, because then you would have the blind leading the blind, and both of you would fall into the ditch.

In the world of Christianity today, there are tens of thousands of teachers, and they are all saying different things. Take ten different Christian teachers, and you will get ten different stories about who God is, how you should worship Him, what salvation is, and how you can be saved.

You don't want your teachers to be spiritually blind. They may be very charming, sincere people, and they may speak with great confidence, but if they are blind, they are still going to lead you into the ditch.

How can you weed out the blind teachers?
How can you find a teacher who can actually see?
How can you stay out of the ditch?

I propose a simple test. *Let us check the accuracy of the Bibles that they use.* For this purpose, we can return to the hypothetical scenario posed at the beginning of this chapter:

If you were faced with a hundred different Bible teachers, you might become frustrated and confused, trying to figure out which teachers are trustworthy, and which teachers are just blind guides.

But suppose that these teachers all used different versions of the Bible. You begin to look at them carefully, and ninety-nine of these Bibles have verses in them which say, "Jesus is a liar." Only one Bible says that you can trust what Jesus says. Would that help you narrow down the playing field? Would you trust any teacher who uses a false Bible? Or would you rather put your trust in the one, solitary teacher who has an accurate copy of the Scriptures?

In Luke 4, Jesus talks about healing the blind, and He quotes from the 61st chapter of Isaiah. We know that Jesus is trustworthy. We can trust that He quoted Isaiah accurately.

But when we review various versions of the Bible, are they in agreement with what Jesus said? Or are there certain copies of Scripture which would make Jesus out to be a liar?

Isaiah 61 – According to Jesus

Let's compare Isaiah 61 in various versions of the Bible:

King James	**NIV**	**Orthodox Study Bible**
The Spirit of the Lord God is upon me; because the Lord hath anointed me to preach good tidings unto the meek; he hath sent me to bind up the brokenhearted, to proclaim liberty to the captives, and the opening of the prison to them that are bound; to proclaim the acceptable year of the Lord . . . (Isaiah 61:1-2)	The Spirit of the Sovereign Lord is on me, because the Lord has anointed me to proclaim good news to the poor. He has sent me to bind up the brokenhearted, to proclaim freedom for the captives and release from darkness for the prisoners, to proclaim the year of the Lord's favor . . . (Isaiah 61:1-2)	The Spirit of the Lord is upon Me, because of which He anointed Me. He sent Me to proclaim good news to the poor, to heal the brokenhearted, to preach liberty to the captives **and recovery of sight to the blind**; to declare the acceptable year of the Lord . . . (Isaiah 61:2)

According to the Orthodox Study Bible, Isaiah prophesied that the Messiah would restore sight to blind people. But in the KJV and NIV, this prophecy says nothing about healing the blind. It is easy to see which version of Scripture is trustworthy, when we see how Jesus himself quoted from the prophet Isaiah:

King James	**NIV**	**Orthodox Study Bible**
And there was delivered unto him the book of the prophet Esaias. And when he had opened the book, he found the place where it was written,	And the scroll of the prophet Isaiah was handed to him. Unrolling it, he found the place where it is written:	And He was handed the book of the prophet Isaiah. And when He had opened the book, He found the place where it was written:
The Spirit of the Lord is upon me, because he hath anointed me to preach the gospel to the poor; he hath sent me to heal the brokenhearted, to preach deliverance to the captives, and **recovering of sight to the blind**, to set at liberty them that are bruised, to preach the acceptable year of the Lord.	"The Spirit of the Lord is on me, because he has anointed me to proclaim good news to the poor. He has sent me to proclaim freedom for the prisoners and **recovery of sight for the blind**, to set the oppressed free, to proclaim the year of the Lord's favor."	"The Spirit of the LORD is upon Me, Because He has anointed Me To preach the gospel to the poor; He has sent Me to heal the brokenhearted, to proclaim liberty to the captives and **recovery of sight to the blind**, to set at liberty those who are oppressed; to proclaim the acceptable year of the LORD."
And he closed the book, and he gave it again to the minister, and sat down. And the eyes of all them that were in the synagogue were fastened on him. And he began to say unto them,	Then he rolled up the scroll, gave it back to the attendant and sat down. The eyes of everyone in the synagogue were fastened on him. He began by saying to them,	Then He closed the book, and gave it back to the attendant and sat down. And the eyes of all who were in the synagogue were fixed on Him. And He began to say to them,
This day is this scripture fulfilled in your ears.	"Today this scripture is fulfilled in your hearing."	"Today this Scripture is fulfilled in your hearing."
(Luke 4:17-21)	(Luke 4:17-21)	(Luke 4:17-21)

The book of Isaiah prophesies of Jesus Christ, telling us that one of His defining characteristics will be His ability to heal the blind. Yet, according to the King James Version, this prophecy is nowhere to be found in this passage from Isaiah. Likewise, in the New International Version, this passage from Isaiah never mentions it. Was Jesus confused? Was the Son of God misquoting Scripture?

Of course not. Jesus was not confused, and it would be silly to suggest that the Son of God would misquote the Scriptures which He Himself inspired. If Jesus reads a passage from the book of Isaiah, then we can rest assured that He is providing an accurate quote from the Old Testament.

But if the words of Jesus are accurate, that means there are inaccuracies in the book of Isaiah, in both the KJV and the NIV. Those versions of the Bible have attempted to change the Word of God.

Unanimously, every version of the New Testament agrees that the Orthodox Study Bible contains the correct reading from the book of Isaiah.

And as we already saw earlier:

- In Romans 3, the apostle Paul quotes from Psalm 14. Yet when you check Psalm 14 in the KJV and NIV, that full quotation is nowhere to be found. In the book of Psalms, only the OSB gets it right.

- In Ephesians 4, the apostle Paul quotes from Psalm 4. Yet the KJV and the NIV do not have this quotation. Only the OSB gets it right.

- The book of Hebrews quotes from Psalm 40, where the incarnation of Jesus Christ is prophesied. Yet in the KJV and NIV, this prophesy is nowhere to be found. Only the OSB gets it right.

- In the book of Acts, Deacon Stephen quotes from Genesis 46. Yet in the KJV and NIV versions of Genesis, this quote can't be found. Only the OSB gets it right.

- In 1 Peter, the apostle Peter quotes from Isaiah 53. But the KJV and NIV versions of Isaiah read differently. Only the OSB gets it right.

- In the book of Romans the apostle Paul quotes from the 10th chapter of Isaiah. But the KJV and NIV do not have this quotation. Only the OSB gets it right.

There are many, many other examples that can be given, where people in the New Testament quote passages from the Old Testament, and the Orthodox Study Bible is the only Bible containing the correct Old Testament reading.

So, who are the blind guides? Who are the false teachers?

If we accept the KJV, the NIV, or any other mainstream Protestant version of the Bible, we would have to conclude that the apostle Paul was mistaken, Stephen was inaccurate, Peter was confused, and Jesus was lying. That is the logical result of accepting a Protestant copy of the Scriptures.

But if we accept the Orthodox Study Bible, we are not faced with these difficulties. When St. Paul quotes from the Psalms, you can actually look in the book of Psalms, and find what he was quoting. When St. Peter quotes from Isaiah, you can read the book of Isaiah, and find the verse he was referring to. And when Jesus himself quotes from Scripture, you can read the passage He was quoting from, and it actually matches what Jesus says in the 4th chapter of Luke.

The Bibles are different from each other, because they are translated from different sources. Historically, the Orthodox Church has always accepted the copy of Scripture which is known as the "Septuagint", and the Orthodox Study Bible has been translated from this ancient source. Meanwhile, Protestants have consistently accepted the copy of Scripture which is known as the "Masoretic Text". These two versions of Scripture do not agree with each other. When Jesus and the apostles quote Scripture in the New Testament, they almost always quote from the Septuagint, not from the Masoretic Text.

So today we are faced with thousands of Christian teachers, all of them competing for your allegiance. So many of them are nice, charming, sincere, and they display great amounts of confidence.

Which teachers are you going to follow? Will you follow the teachers who only use inaccurate Bibles? Or will you follow teachers who recognize the accuracy of the Scriptures as they have been preserved for 2000 years in the Orthodox Church?

Who was Job?

The suffering and the patience of Job are legendary. All ten of his children were killed in a single day, his body was covered with boils, and his soul was vexed by a wife and friends who severely misunderstood him. Yet in the midst of all this, he remained faithful to God, and he never lost his faith.

But who is Job? How is he related to anyone else in all of Scripture? Is he just a lone, solitary soul, with no real connection to anyone else in the entire Bible? Or is there an important connection after all?

Using most translations of Scripture—including the King James Version and the New International Version—there is no way to answer this question. In those versions of the Bible, the last few verses of the book of Job are absent, so his real identity is never fully revealed. We are left with a real admiration of Job, but with no clear understanding of how he was related to anyone else in Scripture. We are left hanging, wanting to know the rest of the story.

In fact, Job was a direct descendant of Abraham! His story fits perfectly into the Scriptures, because the story of God working with Abraham ties directly into how God worked with Job, a great-great-great-grandson of Abraham himself.

Also, it is fascinating to learn that Job wasn't just an average wealthy man. He was a king! Job actually had loyal subjects, and he reigned over a kingdom. But what nation did he reign over? It wasn't Israel!

It turns out that Job isn't the only king mentioned in the book of Job. His three friends—the ones who give him company throughout most of the book—were kings also. That's right: Eliphaz, Bildad, and Zophar weren't just Job's buddies. They were rulers over kingdoms of their own. What kingdoms did they rule over? You can read the King James Version from cover to cover, and you'll never find out. This information is only contained in Bibles which are translated from the Septuagint—Bibles such as the Orthodox Study Bible.

Another surprising fact about Job is that people didn't originally call him Job. When he was younger, he used to go by another name. What name did his momma give him? You'll have to read the OSB to find out.

A particularly beautiful passage is Job 42:18, which explicitly mentions the future resurrection of the body, and prophesies that Job himself will experience that blessed resurrection. Alas, the KJV and the NIV stop short in their versions of the book of Job, leaving us hanging at verse 17.

Let's take some time to compare the last few verses of the book of Job in the KJV, NIV, and the Orthodox Study Bible:

King James	NIV	Orthodox Study Bible
After this lived Job an hundred and forty years, and saw his sons, and his sons' sons, even four generations. So Job died, being old and full of days. (Job 42:16-17)	After this, Job lived a hundred and forty years; he saw his children and their children to the fourth generation. And so Job died, an old man and full of years. (Job 42:16-17)	After this affliction, Job lived one hundred and seventy years, and all the years he lived were two hundred forty-eight; and Job saw his children and grandchildren for four generations. So Job died, old and full of days. **It is written that he will rise with those whom the Lord resurrects.** This man is described in the Syriac book as living in the land of Ausitis, on the borders of Edom and Arabia. **Previously his name was Jobab.** He took an Arabian wife and begot a son named Ennon. But **he himself was the son of his father Zare, one of the sons of Esau,** and of his mother, Bosorra. Thus, **he was the fifth son from Abraham.** Now these were the kings who reigned in Edom, **over which country he also ruled**. First, there was Balak the son of Beor, and the name of his city was Dennaba. But after Balak, there was **Jobab, who is called Job.** After him, there was Asom, who was ruler out of the country of Teman. After him, there was Adad the son of Barad, who destroyed Midian in the plain of Moab; and the name of his city was Gethaim. Now his friends who came to him were: Eliphaz, of the children of Esau, king of the Temanites; Bildad, ruler of the Shuhites; and Zophar, king of the Minians. (Job 42:16-22)

There are some surprising and wonderful gems hidden in this passage from the book of Job. Verse 18 speaks very clearly about the future resurrection of the body! It is also very interesting to note that Job was formerly called "Jobab", that he was a grandson of Esau, and that he was a King over the nation of Edom. **Genesis 36:33 and 1 Chronicles 1:44 both mention Jobab, King of Edom**, testifying to the fact that the Orthodox Study Bible contains an accurate copy of this book.

Of course, when Esau—Job's grandfather—is mentioned in Scripture, it is usually not in very flattering terms. For example:

> And I hated Esau, and laid his mountains and his heritage waste for the dragons of the wilderness. (Malachi 1:3)

> As it is written, Jacob have I loved, but Esau have I hated. (Romans 9:13)

Likewise, Scripture usually looks upon the nation of Edom with a very jaundiced eye. For example:

> he will visit thine iniquity, O daughter of Edom; he will discover thy sins. (Lamentations 4:22)

> I will also stretch out mine hand upon Edom, and will cut off man and beast from it (Ezekiel 25:13)

> Edom shall be a desolate wilderness, for the violence against the children of Judah, because they have shed innocent blood in their land. (Joel 3:19)

> Whereas Edom saith, We are impoverished, but we will return and build the desolate places; thus saith the LORD of hosts, They shall build, but I will throw down; and they shall call them, The border of wickedness, and, The people against whom the LORD hath indignation for ever. (Malachi 1:4)

Thus, if you wanted to be blessed by God, Esau probably wouldn't be your first choice for grandfather, and Edom wouldn't be your first choice for a place to live.

Yet here is Job, a shining example right in the middle of the Bible. He is a grandson of Esau, he is a King of Edom, and he is blessed by God.

This is one of the most important pieces of encouragement we can glean from the final verses of the book of Job. You can know God personally, and you can serve God faithfully, no matter where you live, and no matter who your grandparents are. Even if your ancestors were wicked, you do not have to follow in their footsteps. You can follow God faithfully, and He will accept you, no matter who your relatives happen to be. Thanks be to God!

Where is God in the Book of Esther?

The book of Esther has long been recognized as an enigma in the Protestant Bible, because God is never mentioned anywhere in the entire book. This glaring omission is an embarrassment which has drawn criticism from atheists, agnostics, and even professing Christians.

Robert G. Ingersoll, often called "The Great Agnostic", frequently attempted to discredit the Bible. In one of his published lectures, he said:

> We know that **God is not mentioned or in any way referred to in the book of Esther.** We know, too, that the book is cruel, absurd and impossible. *(Ingersoll, About the Holy Bible, p. 10)*

More recently, the "Scathing Atheist" website offered a similar objection:

> Esther is the final of the "Historical" books and really doesn't belong in the Old Testament at all. Perhaps the most controversial inclusion in the canon, it was not generally accepted as an officially licensed jew-book until after much of the New Testament was written. **It makes no mention of god**, the main character is a woman and it does absolutely nothing to advance the larger story arc of the book. *(http://scathingatheist.com/tag/book-of-esther)*

Many people have questioned this book's inclusion in Scripture. Even today, groups like the Apologetics Press find themselves fielding questions like this:

> Why is the book of Esther in the Bible, since it does not mention God? *(http://www.apologeticspress.org/APPubPage.aspx?pub=1&issue=547&article=74)*

God's apparent absence from the book of Esther has caused many people to question whether God inspired the book at all. Perhaps this was part of the reason why John Calvin never included the book of Esther in his biblical commentaries, and Martin Luther went so far as to say,

> I am so great an enemy to . . . Esther, that I wish [it] had not come to us at all *(Table Talk 24)*

In an exchange with Erasmus, Luther openly claimed that the book of Esther "deserves . . . to be regarded as noncanonical."

Even among those who love the book of Esther, and harbor no hostility, their descriptions of the book can still come across as chilling. Dr. J. Vernon McGee, a popular radio Bible teacher, provides the following comments in his introduction to the book of Esther:

> The Book of Esther in one sense is the most remarkable in the Bible, and that is because **the name of God is not mentioned** in this book at all. There is **not even a divine title or pronoun that refers to God**. Yet the heathen king is mentioned 192 times. **Prayer is not mentioned—it wouldn't be, since God is omitted.**
>
> *(McGee, J. Vernon. Thru the Bible Commentary, Vol. 15: Ezra, Nehemiah & Esther. Nashville, TN: Thomas Nelson Publishers, 1991.)*

Not one mention of God. Not a single reference to prayer. It is easy to understand why many people would find this troubling! And the charge is quite true. In the Protestant version of the book of Esther, no prayers are offered, and God is not mentioned at all.

The King James Version (KJV) and the New International Version (NIV) are no exceptions to this rule. Read the book of Esther from cover to cover, and you will find no reference to God.

Yet, in the Orthodox Study Bible (OSB), the book of Esther does not contain any such omissions. In the very first chapter, God sends Mordecai a prophetic dream regarding his niece, Esther:

> Behold, there was noise and tumult, thunder and earthquake—confusion on the earth. Two great dragons came forth, both ready for combat. A great roar came forth from them, and at the sound of them, every nation prepared to wage war against the nation of the just. And indeed, it was a day of gloom and of darkness, tribulation and anguish, oppression and great confusion upon the earth. The entire upright nation was troubled, fearing the evils against them; they were prepared to perish, **and they cried out to God.** And at their cry there came forth, as it were from a small spring, a great river having abundant water. There was light, and the sun rose, and the lowly were exalted, and they devoured the esteemed. Mordecai, who had seen this vision and **what God was planning to do**, awoke. He kept it in his heart and wished to ponder it until night.
>
> *Nelson, Thomas (2008-02-28). The Orthodox Study Bible: Ancient Christianity Speaks to Today's World (pp. 596-597). Thomas Nelson. Kindle Edition.*

In the very first chapter of the book, we see God mentioned multiple times, we see Him sending a prophetic dream to Mordecai, and the dream includes a vision of people crying out (praying) to God.

In chapter three, Protestant versions of Esther mention that King Artaxerxes sent a letter throughout his kingdom, calling upon his citizens to wipe out the Jewish race. But no copy of the actual letter is provided. In the Orthodox Study Bible, the third chapter of Esther includes a copy of the entire letter, in full.

In chapter four, Protestant versions of Esther contain no prayers.

In the Orthodox Study Bible, the fourth chapter of Esther includes transcripts of magnificent prayers, prayed by both Mordecai and Esther.

The Prayer of Mordecai

He then beseeched the Lord, remembering all the works of the Lord, and said,

> O Lord, Lord, almighty King, all things are under Your power, and there is no one to oppose You in Your desire to save Israel. For You have made heaven and the earth, and every wondrous thing under heaven, and You are the Lord of all, and there is no one who shall resist You, Lord.
>
> You know all things: You know, O Lord, that it is not out of disrespect or arrogance or love of honor that I did this, to refuse to bow down to the haughty Haman, for I would have been happy to kiss the soles of his feet for the salvation of Israel. For I did this in order that I not place the glory of man above the glory of God. I will not bow down to anyone but You, my Lord, and I will not do these things out of arrogance.
>
> And now, O Lord God, King, God of Abraham, save Your people, for they look upon us for our destruction, and they desire to destroy Your inheritance from the beginning. Do not disregard Your portion which You redeemed for Yourself out of the land of Egypt. Hear my prayer and be merciful to Your inheritance. Turn our mourning into feasting so we may live and hymn Your name, O Lord. Do not destroy the mouth of those who praise You.

Then all Israel cried out with all their might, for their death was before their eyes. . . .

The Prayer of Esther

And Queen Esther, seized with the agony of death, fled to the Lord for refuge. And removing her royal garments, she put on the garments of distress and mourning. Instead of the magnificent perfumes, she covered her head with ashes and dirt. She humbled her body exceedingly. She set aside everything of her worldly joy, and her hair was unkempt. She implored the Lord God of Israel, and said:

> O My Lord, You alone are our King. Help me, who am alone and have no help but You! For my risk of danger is in my hand. I have heard from my birth in the tribe of my family that You, O Lord, chose Israel out of all the nations, and our fathers out of all their

ancestors, for an everlasting inheritance, and do for them whatever You have spoken.

Now we sinned before You, and You have delivered us into the hands of our enemies because we have worshiped their gods.

O Lord, You are righteous. But now they are not satisfied with the bitter state of our bondage, but they have pledged to their idols to abolish the decree You have spoken and to destroy Your inheritance, to close the mouths of those who praise You, and to extinguish the glory of Your temple and Your altar, and to open the mouths of the heathen to proclaim the virtues of their false gods, and to extol a human king forever.

O Lord, do not give Your scepter over to those who are not. Do not let them laugh at our fall, but turn their counsel against themselves, and make an example of the one who rules against us.

Remember us, O Lord. Manifest Yourself in the time of our affliction, and encourage me, O King of gods and ruler over every power.

Grant to my mouth proper words in the presence of the lion, to turn his heart to a hatred of our enemy, so that he and those agreeing with him may perish. Save us by Your hand, and help me who am alone and have no one but You, O Lord.

You know all things, and You know I hate the glory of the lawless and abhor the bed of the uncircumcised and of every foreigner. You know my necessity, for I abhor the symbol of my proud station which is upon my head on the days when I appear in public, as if it were a menstrual rag, and I do not wear it on the days I am alone. Your handmaid has not eaten at the table of Haman, nor have I honored the banquet of the king, nor drunk the wine of libations. Neither has Your handmaid rejoiced since the day of her elevation, except in You, O Lord, God of Abraham.

O God, who have power over all, hear the voice of us in despair, and deliver us from the hand of those acting wickedly, and deliver me from my fear.

Nelson, Thomas (2008-02-28). The Orthodox Study Bible: Ancient Christianity Speaks to Today's World (pp. 601-602). Thomas Nelson. Kindle Edition.

These are some of the most moving prayers in all of Scripture. Yet in the Protestant versions of the Bible, they are nowhere to be found. Instead, countless people read the book of Esther in the King James Version (KJV) and New International Version (NIV), and lament that "God is not mentioned" and "prayer is not mentioned". Surely no such objection could be given by those who read the Orthodox book of Esther!

In chapter eight, King Artaxerxes repents of the plot to destroy the Jews, and he publishes a new royal decree, both defending the Jews and honoring their God. Protestant Bibles do not include this letter. The Orthodox Study Bible contains a full copy of the letter, including the following passage:

The New Decree

> ... we find that the Jews, who have been consigned to destruction by this terribly wicked man [Haman], are not criminals, but live by most just laws. We find them to be children of the Most High, Most Mighty, Living God, who has guided the kingdom both for us and our forefathers in the most excellent manner.
>
> Therefore, you will do well to disregard the letters sent by Haman the son of Hammedatha, because he who has produced these has been hanged at the gates of Susa, along with his whole household. For God Almighty, who rules over all things, swiftly rendered a just judgment on him.
>
> Therefore, post a copy of this document publicly in every place, making it known that the Jews are to follow their own customs; and join in supporting them, so that on the day set for their destruction, the thirteenth day of the twelfth month Adar, they may defend themselves against those who would attack them.
>
> For God, who holds power over all things, has made this a day of gladness for them instead of a day of the destruction of a chosen race. Therefore, celebrate this outstanding day among your named feasts with all rejoicing ...
>
> *Nelson, Thomas (2008-02-28). The Orthodox Study Bible: Ancient Christianity Speaks to Today's World (pp. 605-606). Thomas Nelson. Kindle Edition.*

This is truly a remarkable passage of Scripture, for it is one of the few places in the Bible where a pagan king publicly declares the glory of God. It is comparable to the fourth chapter of Daniel, where King Nebuchadnezzar repents of his pride, and openly praises the God of heaven.

In the Protestant version of the book of Esther, the tenth chapter contains no reference to God. Even at the book's close, not a word is said to praise Him.

In the Orthodox book of Esther, chapter ten contains an interpretation of the dream which God had prophetically granted to Mordecai back in the first chapter of the book. According to this passage of Scripture, Mordecai said,

> These things were from my God. For I recall the dream which I had concerning these things, and not one detail of them has failed.
>
> There was a small spring that became a river; there was light and the sun and much water. The river is Esther, whom the king married and made queen. The two serpents are Haman and I. The nations are the

Gentiles gathering together to destroy the name of the Jews. And my nation, which cried out to God and was delivered, is Israel. For the Lord has saved His people, and the Lord has rescued us from all these evils.

And God performed signs and great wonders, which have not happened among the Gentiles. On account of this, He made two lots, one for the people of God and one for the Gentiles. And these two lots came in the hour, and in the time, and in the day of judgment before God and among all the Gentiles.

And God remembered His people and vindicated His inheritance. And they shall observe these days in the month of Adar, the fourteenth and fifteenth day of that month. They shall gather together with joy and gladness before God throughout all generations forever among His people Israel.

Nelson, Thomas (2008-02-28). The Orthodox Study Bible: Ancient Christianity Speaks to Today's World (pp. 607-608). Thomas Nelson. Kindle Edition.

What a wonderful finale to the book! God's prophecy is fulfilled, God's people are miraculously saved, and they give Him the glory, rejoicing in His presence. This is a far cry from the KJV and NIV versions of Esther, where God is never mentioned at all.

When we consider the complete book of Esther, with nothing left out, it is impressive to see how the entire story glorifies God from beginning to end:

- God sends a dream to his prophet, Mordecai.
- God predicts great danger to His people.
- God promises great deliverance to His people.
- The prophet Mordecai prays to God in faith.
- Queen Esther prays to God in faith.
- God performs great signs and wonders, and delivers His people.
- God's prophecy is fulfilled.
- The story ends with God's people gathering together before Him, with joy and gladness.

But in the Protestant version of this book, there is no prophecy, no prayer, and not one reference to God.

Evicting Martyrs from the Hall of Faith

One of the most beloved passages of Scripture is the "Hall of Faith" in the eleventh chapter of Hebrews. In an extensive list of Old Testament saints, honor is given to one hero after another. Abel, Enoch, Noah, Abraham, Sarah, Isaac, Jacob, Joseph, Moses, Rahab, David, Samuel, and many others are mentioned.

Hebrews 11 also refers to many saints by description, rather than by name. Shadrach, Meshach, and Abednego "quenched the violence of fire," and Daniel "stopped the mouths of lions". The widow of Zarephath is one of the "women [who] received their dead raised to life again." The descriptions provided make it easy to tell which saints are being discussed.

Without exception, every saint mentioned in Hebrews 11 is a biblical character. These are all people we can read about in the Holy Scriptures.

This passage mentions faithful martyrs who "were tortured, not accepting deliverance, that they might obtain a better resurrection." (Hebrews 11:35b)

Unfortunately, in many copies of the bible, these martyrs are nowhere to be found. In the entire Protestant Old Testament, there is not a single case where people were tortured because of their faith, and then refused deliverance when it was offered to them. In the KJV and NIV, no one endures torture for the sake of obtaining a better resurrection.

This particular biblical reference can be found in the Orthodox Study Bible, in the book of 2 Maccabees.

In the 2nd century B.C., Antiochus Epiphanes set up an idol of Zeus inside the Jerusalem temple, and he defiled the altar so that no Jewish sacrifices could be performed. In direct violation of God's law for the Jews, Antiochus required everyone to eat pork, and disobedience was punishable by death.

Solomonia and her seven sons were determined to remain faithful to God, and they refused to eat pork. In response, Antiochus had each of her children brutally tortured, and he forced her to watch:

> It came about also that seven brothers with their mother were arrested and forced by the king to be bound and tortured with whips and cords until they partook of the unlawful swine's flesh.
>
> One of them, acting as spokesman, said, "What do you intend to ask and learn from us? For we are ready to die rather than transgress the laws of our fathers."
>
> The king became enraged, and commanded that pans and caldrons be heated. These were heated immediately; and he commanded them to cut out the spokesman's tongue, and to scalp him and cut off his hands and feet, while the rest of the brothers and the mother watched.

> When he was utterly helpless, the king ordered them to take him to the fire, while he was still breathing, and to fry him in a pan. As the smoke from the pan spread out broadly, the brothers and their mother encouraged one another to die bravely, saying, "The Lord God is taking notice of us and in truth is encouraging us, as Moses proclaimed in his song which he sang, bearing witness against the people to their faces: 'And God will have compassion on His servants.'" (2 Maccabees 7:1-6)

The wicked king continued to torture and kill each of her sons, one right after the other, while this innocent mother was watching. They could have escaped torture and execution, simply by obeying the king and eating pork. But these faithful martyrs refused to be released from their tortures, because they had faith in God, and they were looking forward to the resurrection of the righteous:

> The mother was especially admirable and worthy of good memory. Though she saw her seven sons perish in the span of a single day, she bore it courageously because of her hope in the Lord.
>
> She encouraged each of them in the language of their fathers. Filled with a noble spirit, she stirred her womanly reasoning with manly courage, saying to them,
>
> "I do not know how you came into being in my womb. It was not I who gave you breath and life, nor I who arranged in order the elements within each of you. **Therefore the Creator of the world, who formed man in the beginning and devised the origin of all things, will give both breath and life back to you again in His mercy, since you now disregard yourselves for the sake of His laws."** (2 Maccabees 7:20-23)

Six of her sons had been executed before her very eyes, and the time had come for her seventh son to endure the same tortures. Antiochus goes to great lengths, offering the young man a reprieve, hoping that he will disobey God in exchange for his release. But his offers of bribery failed. Thus, he even tried to gain the mother as an ally, hoping that she would convince her son to seek release:

> Antiochus supposed that he was being treated with contempt, and suspected her speech was insulting him personally.
>
> Thus, since the youngest brother was still alive, not only did he appeal to him in words, but at the same time guaranteed him with oaths that he would make him rich and enviable if he would turn away from his fathers, and that he would consider him a friend and entrust him with public affairs. But when the young man refused to pay any attention to him, the king called his mother to him and urged her to advise the boy to save himself. (2 Maccabees 7:24-25)

Solomonia and her sons refused to be released from the tortures. They did not accept deliverance, because they wanted to obtain a better resurrection. They wanted to participate in the resurrection of the righteous:

> After much urging from him, she agreed to persuade her son. But she leaned close to him and mocked the cruel tyrant, speaking in their native tongue, saying, "My son, have mercy on me. I carried you for nine months in my womb, and nursed you for three years. I reared you and brought you up to this point in your life, and have taken care of you. I beseech you, my child, to look at heaven and earth and see everything in them, and know that God made them out of nothing; so also He made the race of man in this way. Do not fear this executioner! But **be worthy of your brothers and accept death, that in God's mercy I may receive you back again with your brothers.**"
>
> While she continued speaking, the young man said to the king, "What are you waiting for? I will not obey the king's command, but I obey the command of the law, given to our fathers through Moses. **But you, who have invented all manner of evil against the Hebrews, will not escape the hands of God**, for we are suffering because of our own sins. So if for the sake of reproof and discipline, our living Lord is angry for a little while, He will again be reconciled with His own servants.
>
> But you, O unholy man and most defiled of all men, do not be elated in vain and puffed up by uncertain hopes when you raise your hand against the children of heaven. You have not yet escaped the judgment of the almighty, all-seeing God. **For now our brothers have endured a brief suffering and then passed on into everlasting life under God's covenant. But you, by God's judgment, will receive just punishments for your haughtiness.** (2 Maccabees 7:26-36)

Solomonia and her sons knew there would be two types of resurrection: the resurrection of the wicked, and the resurrection of the righteous. When the wicked are resurrected, it will be unto judgment, but when the righteous are resurrected, it will be unto life eternal. They wanted a good resurrection. They wanted no part in the judgment which would eventually come down upon this wicked king, Antiochus.

Hebrews 11:35 mentions this story from the Old Testament. It speaks of these faithful people who "were tortured, not accepting deliverance, that they might obtain a better resurrection."

Even though the book of Hebrews refers to these biblical saints of old, they cannot be found anywhere in the KJV or the NIV. Thankfully, we can read about them in the Orthodox Study Bible.

Erasing a Prophecy of Christ

Years before Jesus was born, the Holy Spirit inspired one of His prophets to tell the future, and to write down some things which had not happened yet. In this prophecy, we hear about someone who claims to be the Son of God, and is tortured, and is condemned to a shameful death. This prophecy is written from the perspective of those who condemn Christ. Many years before they are even born, we get to hear the internal thought processes of the Pharisees. Here is the prophecy itself, word-for-word from the Old Testament:

> Let us lie in ambush for the righteous man, because he is useless to us and opposes our deeds; he denounces us for our sins against the law and accuses us of sins against our upbringing. He claims to have knowledge of God, and he calls himself a child of the Lord. He has become for us as a refutation of our purposes; even seeing him is a burden to us, because his life is unlike that of others; for his paths go in a different direction. We are considered by him as a hybrid, and he avoids our ways as something immoral.
>
> He considers the last things of the righteous as blessed and pretends that God is his Father. Let us see if his words are true, and let us put these last things to the test at the end of his life. For if the righteous man is a son of God, He will help him, and deliver him from the hand of those who oppose him.
>
> Let us test him with insult and torture that we may know his gentleness and test his patient endurance. Let us condemn him to a shameful death, for there shall be a visitation because of his words.

This is one of my favorite prophecies of Jesus, because of its incredible clarity. It is almost as if we have secretly wiretapped a meeting place for the religious leaders of ancient Israel, and are actually listening in on the Pharisees as they plot the murder of Jesus. Written many years before Jesus was even born, this striking prophecy predicts that the Messiah would claim to be the Son of God, that he would chastise the religious leaders for their lawlessness and hypocrisy, and that the religious leaders would condemn him to a shameful death.

This prophecy includes some of the specific thought processes which the Pharisees display in the New Testament. Consider the following passage from the book of Matthew:

> Likewise the chief priests also, mocking with the scribes and elders, said, "He saved others; Himself He cannot save. If He is the King of Israel, let Him now come down from the cross, and we will believe

Him. He trusted in God; let Him deliver Him now if He will have Him; for He said, 'I am the Son of God.'"

This passage can be found in Matthew 27:41-43. And it is a very specific fulfillment of the Old Testament prophecy we looked at earlier. In the prophecy, the Pharisees say, *"For if the righteous man is a son of God, He will help him, and deliver him from the hand of those who oppose him."* They are focusing on Jesus' claim to be God's son, and they suggest that God should save him from death if his claim is true. Likewise, in Matthew 27, the Pharisees mockingly say that God should deliver Jesus from death, since Jesus claimed to be the Son of God.

These sorts of prophecies demonstrate the fact that the Scriptures are inspired by the Holy Spirit. On his own, man is not able to predict the future like this. So when we read prophecies like this one, written many years before the actual events ever took place, we are able to see the very signature of God.

In Scripture, God announces that He stands alone in the universe. He alone has the ability to declare what will come to pass in the future. In Isaiah 46:9-10, we read the following:

> I am God, and there is no other;
> I am God, and there is none like Me,
> Declaring the end from the beginning,
> And from ancient times
> things that are not yet done,
> Saying, "My counsel shall stand,
> And I will do all My pleasure"

In prophecies such as the one we read earlier, we can clearly see the fingerprints of God:

- Years before the birth of Jesus, how could anyone have known that the Messiah would chastise the religious leaders of Israel, and that they would be the ones to condemn him to a shameful death?
- How could anyone know that the Messiah would claim to be the Son of God?
- Many years before the events ever happened, how did the author of this Old Testament prophecy write down something that would eventually be fulfilled in the 27th chapter of the book of Matthew?

There is no reasonable explanation for this, except for the inspiration of Scripture. There is no way to explain this, except to submit to the majesty of our omniscient God, who knows all, and who declares the end from the beginning.

Prophecies like this help strengthen our confidence in the Scriptures, as we recognize that the words of the Bible are the very words of God. God left His signature on Scripture, setting it apart from all other books in the world.

With all of this in mind, think about your own home. Imagine that just across the street, in easy walking distance from your own front door, a grand, beautiful, magnificent new church is built. Before you even leave your own front yard, you are in awe of this incredible architectural work of art. The very sight of this new church fills you with wonder, and lifts your thoughts to Heaven.

Intrigued, you decide to investigate this church for yourself. You want to find out whether this church is as impressive on the inside, as it is on the outside. You barely make it through the front doors of the church, and you are nearly swarmed with friendly people. This is not the work of a professional greeter – a guy who stands near the door greeting you because that's his job – this is person after person simply being friendly. One after the other, they walk up to you with a smile, shake your hand, introduce themselves, and they show a genuine interest in getting to know you better. This is definitely the warmest, friendliest church you have ever visited in your life!

You take your place in the pew, and you wait to see what the worship service is like. You are blown away by the sheer majesty and beauty of the music. The singers and musicians are all extremely talented, and are very impressive. Yet they perform in such a way that they don't draw attention to themselves individually. The music is beautiful, and it is all directed to the glory of God. When you hear the music, and when you sing along, your thoughts and your heart are again drawn up into Heaven itself.

The sermon is just as impressive. The pastor's voice is pleasant, his stories hold your attention, and you agree wholeheartedly with the message itself. He does such a good job that you decide to get a recorded copy of the sermon, so you can listen to it again, and then pass it along to your friends.

After the service, you get up to leave, expecting everyone to race out the door in a hurry. But one of your new friends in the congregation stops you, and invites you to the most delicious Sunday luncheon you have ever attended. The sheer variety of mouthwatering food makes you feel like you have stumbled into the banquet of a great king. There are tender roasts, perfectly seasoned hams, casseroles, stews, soups, and some of the richest chocolate desserts you have ever tasted. You ask what the special occasion is, and you friend tells you, "We enjoy this same sort of fellowship meal every single week, right after church."

Truly, to say this church has impressed you would be an understatement. Everything seems almost too perfect. Everything about this church, from the people, to the music, to the sermon, to the banquet, all make you want to come back again for more.

Over the next several weeks, you continue attending, and you are not disappointed. With a regularity that amazes you, this wonderful church consistently provides you with what you feel is the perfect worship experience. Your every desire is fulfilled. Every Sunday, without fail, you love the music, you love the food, you love the sermon, and most of all, you love the friendly people.

But then one Sunday you have a very strange experience. At this otherwise perfect church, you encounter something which is so bizarre, that you never even dreamed it would have needed investigation.

That morning, you had been in a hurry, and you accidentally left your Bible at home. Initially, it seemed to be no problem, since there are Bibles available for everyone at church. After walking into the church and saying hello to a couple of your friends, you pick up one of the Bibles, and you take your seat. While the pastor is preaching, you flip open to the passage he is talking about, and you read along. The sermon is impressive as usual, and for the moment, you don't notice anything strange.

But then after the service is over, you decide to flip over to read one of your favorite passages of Scripture. The 23rd Psalm comforts you every time you read it. *"The Lord is my Shepherd, I shall not want. He makes me to lie down in green pastures. He leads me beside still waters. . . ."* But as you turn the pages of this Bible, you become very confused. You find the book of Job, and the book of Ecclesiastes, but in between them, there is no book of Psalms, and there is no book of Proverbs! Your first thought is that some kid tore out the pages. But when you look closely, you don't see any evidence that the book has been damaged in any way. Then you think, *"Maybe this Bible doesn't put books in the same order as usual . . . maybe it's ordered chronologically, or something like that."* So you flip over to the table of contents, to figure out where the Psalms are. To your amazement, you discover that the book of Psalms is not listed anywhere in the table of contents either. Neither is the book of Proverbs. It is as if all the Psalms and all the Proverbs simply disappeared from the Bible, without leaving a trace!

You start flipping through this unusual Bible to see whether it is missing anything else. Thankfully, the book of Genesis is intact. It would be odd indeed if the first book of the Bible was missing. Exodus is also there. But as you continue turning pages, you discover that the book of Psalms is not the only book of Scripture which is missing from this Bible. You find that the books of Joshua and Judges are there, but the book of Ruth is missing. You remember it is the story of a beautiful Moabite woman who became a widow and almost lost everything, but then married a kind and wealthy landowner named Boaz, and they became the great-grandparents of King David. This book contains one of the most beautiful love stories in all of Scripture, and you are saddened to discover that it is missing from this Bible.

You turn further, and you are shocked to see that the book of Isaiah is missing! This really bothers you, because you know that many of the Old Testament prophecies about Jesus are in the book of Isaiah. Then you look for John 3:16 — your favorite verse in the Bible — and your jaw drops when you see that the Gospel of John is missing too. Matthew, Mark, and Luke are there, but not John. You are happy to see that the book of Acts is there, but the book of Romans is gone. You turn further, and find that most of the books are still there, but several are missing. Even the book of Revelation is gone! All those prophecies of Christ's return, all those magnificent descriptions of the incense, robes, and singing in Heaven . . . gone without a trace. What in the world is going on?!?

At this point, you are convinced that there must have been some sort of enormous, unbelievable printing error. There must have been some massive, inexplicable computer error at the publishing company, and they must have released a defective Bible by sheer accident. Surely, all their Bibles could not have been printed the same way, or else everybody in the church would notice! The solution was obvious . . . just throw away this bad Bible, and use one of the others.

So, you pitch that bizarre Bible in the trash where it belongs, and you get a couple others. And this is where you really start scratching your head, because both of these Bibles match the first one! The Psalms and Proverbs are missing. So are the books of Ruth, Isaiah, the Gospel of John, Romans, Revelation, and two other books. Altogether, there are nine books that are missing from these Bibles, and there is no explanation that you can imagine. Why in the world were all these incomplete Bibles printed, and how in the world did they end up in this church?

Frustrated and confused, you find one of your new friends at the church, and you explain what you have discovered. You ask, *"Why are these Bibles incomplete? Scripture says that it is a sin to take away from God's Word, so why are there 9 books missing from all these Bibles? What happened?"*

Your friend smiles, laughs, and doesn't act surprised at all. But you are shocked by what you hear. Your friend's response is this: *"We had those Bibles printed that way on purpose. At our church, we do not believe that those particular 9 books are Scripture at all. They are good books, but they are not the Word of God. We believe that there are only 57 books in the Bible. That's why we left out those other books."*

At this point, you are reeling, and you almost feel dizzy. You feel warm blood rushing to your head, and you start to feel angry. How could anyone deny that the book of Isaiah is part of the Bible? It contains so many prophecies about Jesus! How could anyone leave out the book of Proverbs? What about John, Romans, and Revelation? How could you call a book "the Bible" if it is missing all these books? How could God possibly be pleased by this?

Please think carefully for a minute. Imagine that all of this actually happened to you. Imagine that you had been faithfully attending a beautiful church with magnificent music, excellent preaching, and friendly people. Imagine that you enjoyed everything about the church, and that you had no complaints at all. As far as you can remember, this is the most perfect church you have ever attended in your life. But then you discover these incomplete Bibles. After some investigation, you find out that all the Bibles in this church are missing 9 books. If you become a member of this church, you will have to agree that Psalms, Proverbs, Isaiah, Ruth, John, Romans, Revelation, and two other books are not the Word of God. You will have to get rid of your old Bible, and you will have to get one of these new Bibles that only has 57 books in it.

If this happened to you, what would you do? Would you keep going to this church? Would you get one of these new Bibles? Would you be willing to lose 9 books of Scripture?

If you are like many people, you would leave this church quickly, and you would never return. No matter how beautiful the church building is, no matter how incredible the music sounds, no matter how much you enjoy the sermons, and no matter how friendly the people are, you would not be willing to sacrifice your Bible. No matter how much you love that church, you would not go there, if they forced you to tear 9 books out of your Bible. You cannot bear to pretend that these books are not Scripture, inspired by the Holy Spirit. No matter how good this church seems to be in other ways, you just cannot accept its incomplete Bible. It is just not worth it.

This may surprise you, but there are many churches which are just like the one described in this story. On the outside, they seem wonderful. The architecture is beautiful. The people are friendly. The music is excellent. The preaching is exciting. And even the food is good. But once you open up a Bible in one of these churches, you will find that many Scriptures have disappeared.

The Psalms and Proverbs are still there. So is Ruth, and so is the book of Isaiah. These Bibles are not missing the Gospel of John. The book of Acts is still in place, and nobody has forgotten about the book of Revelation. But other books are missing.

Remember the amazing Old Testament prophecy we read earlier? That prophecy was written in the century before Jesus was born, and it includes many specific details about His life. This prophecy tells us that Jesus would claim to be the Son of God, that Jesus would criticize the religious leaders for being hypocrites, and that they would condemn Him to a shameful death. An important part of the prophecy is a direct prediction of what the Pharisees said in the New Testament, in Matthew 27:43. This particular part of the prophecy is important, because *it is the only prediction of Matthew 27:43 which can be found in the entire Old Testament.*

But if you walk into most churches in America, and you check their Bibles, you will not find this prophecy anywhere. *It has been erased.*

This prophecy of Jesus can be found in the Old Testament, in the book of Wisdom, chapter 2, verses 12-20. For the first 1,500 years of the Church, it was easy to find this prophecy, because the book of Wisdom was widely accepted as Scripture throughout the worldwide Church. From the time of the apostles, until the 16th century, the book of Wisdom was understood to be a part of Scripture, inspired by the Holy Spirit. When people considered the prophecy of Christ that is contained in the book of Wisdom, they recognized it as the signature of God . . . every bit as much as the prophecies of Christ which are contained in the book of Isaiah, or the Psalms.

But then something tragic happened during the Protestant Reformation. As Martin Luther, Ulrich Zwingli, John Calvin, and other early Protestants fought against the sins of the 16th century Catholic Church, they threw out the baby with the bathwater. Even though there were some abuses in the Catholic Church which needed to be corrected, the Protestant Reformers made the enormous mistake of removing several books from the Bible, which had been considered Scripture since the time of the apostles.

Over the next century, most Protestants still included these books of Scripture in their Bibles. Even the original 1611 King James Version of the Bible included the book of Wisdom, the book of Tobit, the book of Baruch, and several others.

The first Protestant Bible ever printed with 66 books was the 1599 Geneva Bible. For 1,598 years, the worldwide Church was content to recognize the signature God had placed on books such as Wisdom, Tobit, and Sirach. But then in the year 1599, Protestants decided it was time to try something new. At the last minute, they instructed the publisher to leave several of the books unprinted. The result was the 1599 Geneva Bible, which included 66 books, and also included scores of blank pages, where the other books were originally intended to be printed. I wish that Protestant Bibles were still printed this way; at least the blank pages would serve as a reminder that something has been taken away from us.

Thankfully, not all churches have been willing to accept this shortened Bible. Even today, there are many churches you can attend where the Bibles are not missing all these books.

For example, consider the Old Testament book of Wisdom. If you walk into an Orthodox Church, or into a Catholic Church, you will find Bibles which still contain this book of Scripture. And on the Protestant side of the fence, you can also find a number of Anglicans who realize that the book of Wisdom bears the very signature of God. The prophecies of Christ contained therein cannot be the product of mere men.

If you want to know where your church stands, simply open up one of its Bibles. See whether it contains the following nine books:
- Tobit (*Tobias*)
- Judith
- 1 Maccabees
- 2 Maccabees
- 3 Maccabees
- Wisdom of Solomon (*Wisdom*)
- Wisdom of Sirach (*Ecclesiasticus*)
- Baruch
- Epistle of Jeremiah

If your Bible contains all of these books, you can breathe a sigh of relief. But if that Bible is missing some of its books, then run away. Run fast. You should own a Bible that contains all the books of Scripture. You need a copy of the Bible which still bears the full *signature of God.*

The original 1611 King James Version (KJV) contained the book of Wisdom, but it was later removed. Today, the KJV is missing this book. Likewise, the New International Version (NIV) does not have the book of Wisdom.

The Orthodox Study Bible includes the book of Wisdom. Thankfully, this prophecy of Christ has not been lost.

Where Did All These Differences Come From?

As we have seen above, the King James Version (KJV) and New International Version (NIV) are missing many passages which can be found in the Orthodox Study Bible (OSB). When we check the New Testament to see how Jesus and the apostles quote the Old Testament, we consistently find that the Orthodox Study Bible is accurate, while the KJV and NIV often come up short.

And we have barely even scratched the surface! There are many more passages we could consider, where New Testament quotations favor the Orthodox Study Bible, but do not match the KJV and NIV.

The New Testament favors the Septuagint over the Masoretic Text approximately 13-to-1. In one particular study, R. Grant Jones identified 78 instances where the New Testament quotes the Old Testament, favoring the Septuagint over the Masoretic, and a mere 6 instances where the quotation favored the Masoretic over the Septuagint. That tips the scales 93% in favor of the Septuagint. Thus, it is not difficult to identify what copy of the Scriptures Jesus and the apostles were reading.

The differences between various versions of the Bible can make a person's head spin. Where did all of these differences come from? What is the cause of all this confusion?

The primary answer to this question concerns two different texts of Scripture. One group of texts, written in Hebrew, is called the "Masoretic Text". Another group of texts, written in Greek, is called the "Septuagint".

When people translate the ancient texts into English, which source do they use? For 2000 years, since the time of the apostles, the Orthodox Church has always recognized the Septuagint as being accurate. But Protestants, for the past 500 years, have usually chosen to translate their Bibles from the Masoretic Text.

I used to believe the Masoretic Text was a perfect copy of the original Old Testament. I used to believe that the Masoretic Text was how God divinely preserved the Hebrew Scriptures throughout the ages.

I was wrong.

The oldest copies of the Masoretic Text only date back to the 10th century, nearly 1000 years *after* the time of Christ. And these texts differ from the originals in many specific ways. The Masoretic text is named after the Masoretes, who were scribes and Torah scholars who worked in the middle-east between the 7th and 11th centuries. The texts they received, and the edits they provided, ensured that the modern Jewish texts would manifest a notable departure from the original Hebrew Scriptures.

Historical research reveals five significant ways in which the Masoretic Text is different from the original Old Testament:

1. The Masoretes admitted that they **received corrupted texts** to begin with.

2. The Masoretic Text is written with a **radically different alphabet** than the original.

3. The Masoretes **added vowel points** which did not exist in the original.

4. The Masoretic Text **excluded several books** from the Old Testament scriptures.

5. The Masoretic Text includes **changes to prophecy and doctrine**.

We will consider each point in turn:

Receiving Corrupted Texts

Many people believe that the ancient Hebrew text of Scripture was divinely preserved for many centuries, and was ultimately recorded in what we now call the "Masoretic Text". But what did the Masoretes themselves believe? Did they believe they were perfectly preserving the ancient text? Did they even think they had *received* a perfect text to begin with?

History says "no" . . .

Scribal emendations – Tikkune Soferim

> Early rabbinic sources, from around 200 CE, mention several passages of Scripture in which the conclusion is inevitable that the ancient reading must have differed from that of the present text. . . . Rabbi Simon ben Pazzi (3rd century) calls these readings "emendations of the Scribes" (tikkune Soferim; Midrash Genesis Rabbah xlix. 7), assuming that the Scribes actually made the changes. This view was adopted by the later Midrash and by the majority of Masoretes.[1]

---

[1] http://en.wikipedia.org/wiki/Masoretic_Text#Scribal_emendations_-_Tikkune_Soferim

In other words, *the Masoretes themselves felt they had received a partly corrupted text.*

A stream cannot rise higher than its source. If the texts they *started* with were corrupted, then even a *perfect* transmission of those texts would only serve to preserve the *mistakes*. Even if the Masoretes demonstrated great care when copying the texts, their diligence would not bring about the correction of even one error.

In addition to these *intentional* changes by Hebrew scribes, there also appear to be a number of *accidental* changes which they allowed to creep into the Hebrew text. For example, consider Psalm 145 . . .

Psalm 145 is an acrostic poem. Each line of the Psalm starts with a successive letter of the Hebrew alphabet. Yet in the Masoretic Text, one of the lines is completely missing:

Psalm 145 is an acrostic psalm where each verse begins with the next letter of the Hebrew alphabet. In the Aleppo Codex the first verse begins with the letter aleph, the second with the beyt, the third with the gimel, and so on. Verse 13 begins with the letter מ (mem-top highlighted letter), the 13th letter of the Hebrew alphabet; the next verse begins with the letter ס (samech-bottom highlighted letter), the 15th letter of the Hebrew alphabet. There is no verse beginning with the 14th letter נ (nun).

Yet the Septuagint (LXX) Greek translation of the Old Testament *does* include the missing verse. And when that verse is translated back into Hebrew, it starts with the Hebrew letter נ (nun) which was missing from the Masoretic Text.

In the early 20th century, the Dead Sea Scrolls were discovered in caves near Qumran. They revealed an ancient Hebrew textual tradition which differed from the tradition preserved by the Masoretes. Written in Hebrew, copies of Psalm 145 were found which include the missing verse:

When we examine Psalm 145 from the Dead Sea Scrolls, we find between the verse beginning with the מ (mem-top) and the verse beginning with the ס (samech-bottom), the verse beginning with the letter נ (nun-center). This verse, missing from the Aleppo Codex, and missing from all modern Hebrew Bibles that are copied from this codex, but found in the Dead Sea Scrolls, says נאמן יהוה בדברו וחסיד בכל מעשיו (The Lord is faithful in His words and holy in all His works).

The missing verse reads, *"The Lord is faithful in His words and holy in all His works."* This verse can be found in the Orthodox Study Bible, which relies on the Septuagint. But this verse is absent from the King James Version (KJV), the New King James Version (NKJV), the Douay-Rheims, the Complete Jewish Bible, and every other translation which is based on the Masoretic Text.

In this particular case, it is easy to demonstrate that the Masoretic Text is in error, for it is obvious that Psalm 145 was originally written as an acrostic Psalm. But what are we to make of the *thousands* of other locations where the Masoretic Text diverges from the Septuagint? If the Masoretic Text could completely erase an entire verse from one of the Psalms, how many other passages of Scripture have been edited? How many other verses have been erased?

A Radically Different Alphabet

If Moses were to see a copy of the Masoretic Text, he wouldn't be able to read it. The original Old Testament scriptures were written in Paleo-Hebrew, a text closely related to the ancient Phonecian writing system. The Masoretic Text is written with an alphabet which was borrowed from Assyria (Persia) around the 6th-7th century B.C., and is almost 1000 years *newer* than the form of writing used by Moses, David, and most of the Old Testament authors.

Just imagine . . . You discover a time-machine, you travel back to the year 1425 B.C., and you meet Moses face-to-face. You excitedly tote along your favorite

Hebrew/English interlinar Bible, complete with the Masoretic text and its English translation. You look forward to showing Moses his own writings in print, transported over three thousand years in time.

To your surprise and disappointment, Moses just shrugs at the text, and leers at you with an odd look on his face. You show him the Ten Commandments, yet Moses has no clue how to read it. He gladly acknowledges his encounter with God on Mt. Sinai, but he says this text *looks nothing like what God wrote on those two stone tablets*.

In desperation, you focus on the most important word in the entire Old Testament—The Tetragrammaton—The all-holy four-letter name of God. YHWH. Surely Moses will immediately recognize the Hebrew inscription for God's name!

God's name is shown here in Paleo-Hebrew (top) and in modern Hebrew (bottom). Modern Hebrew letters would have been unrecognizable to Abraham, Moses, David, and most of the authors of the Old Testament.

To your dismay, Moses says this word is just as foreign as everything else you have shown him. Moses writes the Lord's name himself, hoping to teach you the proper way to write it. This word, too, is four letters. But it looks as foreign to you as your text looks to Moses.

You return home, disappointed, but wiser. The next time someone gushes with excitement about the "ancient Hebrew text", and the ability to "read the same words Moses wrote", you don't share their excitement. You hold your peace, and you meditate on God's awesome ability to preserve His Truth from generation to generation, *even if He has not preserved the original text of Scripture.*

Most of the Old Testament scriptures were written in Paleo-Hebrew, or a closely related derivative. Generally considered to be an offshoot of ancient Phonecian script, Paleo-Hebrew represents the pen of David, the script of Moses, *and perhaps even the Finger of God on the stone tablets of the Ten Commandments.*

Modern Hebrew, on the other hand, is not quite so ancient. Israelites acquired this new alphabet from Assyria (Persia), somewhere around the 6th-7th century B.C. This was the same general time period as Israel's exile to Babylon . . . many centuries *after* most of the Old Testament was written.

Initially, the Old Testament Scriptures were exclusively written in Paleo-Hebrew. Then, after borrowing the new alphabet from the Assyrians, the Jews began transliterating large portions of Scripture into the newer version.

~135 A.D. – This coin struck during the Bar Kokhba revolt demonstrates usage of the Paleo-Hebrew alphabet in the early 2nd century.

But old habits die hard. Especially with religion. Especially in regard to the name of God. For a period of time, Jews transcribed the majority of the Old Testament using the new Hebrew alphabet, while retaining the more ancient way of writing God's name. Thus, for a while, the Hebrew Scriptures were written with a mixture of two different alphabets. Even after the Jews began exclusively using the new Assyrian letters to copy the text of Scripture, the more ancient Paleo-Hebrew letters persisted in some corners of Jewish society. As late as the 2nd century A.D., during the Bar Kokhba revolt, Jewish coins displayed writing with the ancient Paleo-Hebrew script.

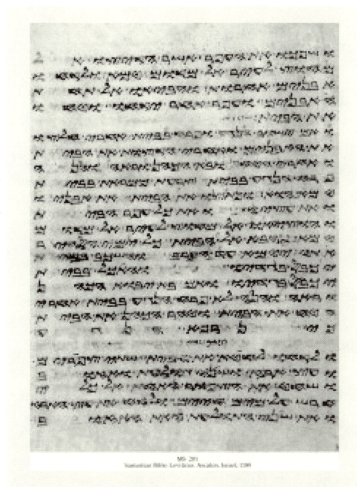

The Samaritan Pentateuch uses the Samaritan alphabet, which is closely related to Paleo-Hebrew. It is likely that much of this text looks similar to what Moses and David saw in the original copies of the Old Testament. The Masoretic Text differs from the Samaritan Pentateuch in over 6,000 places.

Eventually, though, the newer Assyrian alphabet won the day. No new copies were being made of the ancient text, and the earliest copies of Scripture eventually disintegrated. By the time of Christ, the only existing copies of the

Old Testament had either been transliterated into modern Hebrew, or translated into Greek (in the Septuagint). One exception is the Samaritan Pentateuch, which continues to be written in the ancient form, even to this day. However, Jews and Christians both rejected the text as being of questionable accuracy.

Today, many people are under the false impression that the Masoretic Text represents the "original Hebrew", and that the Septuagint is less trustworthy because it is "just a translation". In fact, nothing could be further from the truth. The Septuagint is actually *more faithful to the original Hebrew* than the Masoretic Text is.

We no longer have original copies of the Old Testament.

Nor do we have copies of the originals.

We now have copies of the Scriptures transliterated into modern Hebrew, edited by scribes, compiled by the Masoretes in the 7th-11th centuries, and embellished with modern vowel points which did not exist in the original language. This is what we now call the "Masoretic Text".

We also have copies of the Old Testament Scriptures which were translated into Greek, over 1000 years *earlier* than the oldest existing Masoretic text. During New Testament times, Jesus and the Apostles quoted from this Greek translation frequently, and with full authority. They treated it as the Word of God, and as a faithful translation. This is what we now call the "Septuagint".

Adding Vowel Points

For thousands of years, ancient Hebrew was only written with consonants, no vowels. When reading these texts, they had to supply all of the vowels from memory, *based on oral tradition.*

In Hebrew, just like modern languages, vowels can make a big difference. The change of a single vowel can radically change the meaning of a word. An example in English is the difference between "SLAP" and "SLIP". These words have very different definitions. Yet if our language was written without vowels, both of these words would be written "SLP". Thus the vowels are very important.

The most extensive change the Masoretes brought to the Hebrew text was the addition of "vowel points". In an attempt to solidfy for all-time the "correct" readings of all the Hebrew Scriptures, the Masoretes added a series of dots to the text, identifying which vowel to use in any given location.

Adam Clarke, an 18th Century Protestant scholar, demonstrates that the vowel-point system is actually a running commentary which was incorporated into the text itself. In the General Preface of his biblical commentary published in 1810, Clarke writes:

> The Masorets were the most extensive Jewish commentators which that nation could ever boast. The system of punctuation, probably invented by them, is a continual gloss on the Law and the Prophets; their vowel points, and prosaic and metrical accents, &c., give every word to which they are affixed a peculiar kind of meaning, which in their simple state, multitudes of them can by no means bear. The vowel points alone add whole conjugations to the language. This system is one of the most artificial, particular, and extensive comments ever written on the Word of God; for there is not one word in the Bible that is not the subject of a particular gloss through its influence.

Another early scholar who investigated this matter was Louis Cappel, who wrote during the early 17th century. An article in the 1948 edition of the Encyclopedia Britannica includes the following information regarding his research of the Masoretic Text:

> As a Hebrew scholar, he concluded that the vowel points and accents were not an original part of Hebrew, but were inserted by the Masorete Jews of Tiberias, not earlier then the 5th Century AD, and that the primitive Hebrew characters are Aramaic and were substituted for the more ancient at the time of the captivity... The various readings in the Old Testament Text and the differences between the ancient versions and the Masoretic Text convinced him that the integrity of the Hebrew text as held by Protestants, was untenable.

Many Protestants love the Masoretic Text, believing it to be a trustworthy representation of the original Hebrew text of Scripture. Yet, at the same time, most Protestants reject Orthodox Church Tradition as being untrustworthy. They believe that the Church's oral tradition could not possibly preserve Truth over a long period of time.

Therefore, the vowel points of the Masoretic Text put Protestants in a precarious position. If they believe that the Masoretic vowels are *not* trustworthy, then they call the Masoretic Text itself into question. But if they believe that the Masoretic vowels *are* trustworthy, then they are forced to believe that the Jews successfully preserved the vowels of Scripture for thousands of years, *through oral tradition alone*, until the Masoretes finally invented the vowel points hundreds of years after Christ. Either conclusion is at odds with mainstream Protestant thought.

Either oral tradition can be trusted, or it can't. If it can be trusted, then there is no reason to reject the Traditions of the Orthodox Church, which faithfully have been preserved for nearly 2000 years. But if traditions are always untrustworthy, then the Masoretic vowel points are also untrustworthy, and should be rejected.

Excluding Books of Scripture from the Old Testament

The Masoretic Text promotes a particular canon of the Old Testament which is significantly shorter than the canon represented by the Septuagint. Meanwhile, Orthodox Christians and Catholics have Bibles which incorporate the canon of the Septuagint. The books of Scripture found in the Septuagint, but not found in the Masoretic Text, are commonly called either the *Deuterocanon* or the *anagignoskomena*. While it is outside the scope of this book to perform an in-depth study of the canon of Scripture, a few points relevant to the Masoretic Text should be made here:

- Most of the books in the Deuterocanon were *originally written in Hebrew.*
- In three places, *the Jewish Talmud refers to the book of Sirach as "Scripture".*
- Jesus celebrated[2] Hanukkah, a feast which originates in the Old Testament book of *1 Maccabees.*
- The New Testament book of *Hebrews* recounts the stories of multiple Old Testament saints, including a reference to martyrs in the book of *2 Maccabees.*
- The book of *Wisdom* includes a striking prophecy of Christ, and its fulfillment is recorded in *Matthew 27.*
- Numerous findings among the Dead Sea Scrolls suggest that a number of 1st-century Jewish communities accepted many of the Deuterocanonical books as authentic Scripture.
- Many thousands of 1st-century Christians were converts from Judaism. The early Church accepted the inspiration of the Deuterocanon, and frequently quoted authoritatively from books such as Wisdom, Sirach, and Tobit. This early Christian practice suggests that many Jews had already accepted these books, even prior to their conversion to Christianity.
- Ethiopian Jews preserved the ancient Jewish acceptance of the Septuagint, including much of its canon of Scripture. *Sirach, Judith, Baruch, and Tobit* are among the books included in the canon of Scripture used by modern Ethiopian Jews.

---

[2] Hanukkah is also known as the "Festival of Lights", or the "Feast of the Dedication", and is mentioned in John 10:22-30. How fitting that Jesus—the Light of the world—walked into the temple during the Festival of Lights, and declared himself to be one with the Father!

These reasons, among others, suggest the existence of a large 1st-century Jewish community which accepted the Deuterocanon as inspired Scripture.

Changes to Prophecy and Doctrine

When compiling any given passage of Scripture, the Masoretes had to choose among multiple versions of the ancient Hebrew texts. In some cases the textual differences were relatively inconsequential. For example, two texts may differ over the spelling of a person's name.

However, in other cases they were presented with textual variants which made a considerable impact upon doctrine or prophecy. In cases like these, were the Masoretes completely objective? Or did their anti-Christian biases influence any of their editing decisions?

In the 2nd century A.D., hundreds of years before the time of the Masoretes, Justin Martyr investigated a number of Old Testament texts in various Jewish synagogues.

He ultimately concluded that the Jews who had rejected Christ had also rejected the Septuagint, and were now tampering with the Hebrew Scriptures themselves:

> But I am far from putting reliance in your teachers, who refuse to admit that the interpretation made by the seventy elders who were with Ptolemy [king] of the Egyptians is a correct one; and they attempt to frame another. And I wish you to observe, that they have altogether taken away many Scriptures from the [Septuagint] translations effected by those seventy elders who were with Ptolemy, and by which this very man who was crucified is proved to have been set forth expressly as God, and man, and as being crucified, and as dying
>
> (~150 A.D., Justin Martyr, *Dialogue with Trypho the Jew*, chapter LXXI)

If Justin Martyr's findings are correct, then it is likely that the Masoretes inherited a Hebrew textual tradition which had already been corrupted with an anti-Christian bias. And if we look at some of the most significant differences between the Septuagint and the Masoretic Text, that is precisely what we see. For example, consider the following comparisons:

This passage in the New Testament...	depends on this passage from the Septuagint (LXX) version of the Old Testament...	to show that God had prophecied this...	but the Masoretic Text (MT) reads quite differently...
"when He [Jesus] comes into the world, He says, '... a body you have prepared for me'... we have been sanctified through the offering of the body of Jesus Christ" (Hebrews 10:4-10)	"Sacrifice and offering You did not will; But a body You prepared for me" (Psalm 39:7, Orthodox Study Bible)	The Incarnation	"You desired neither sacrifice nor meal offering; You dug ears for me" (Psalm 40:7, Complete Jewish Bible)
"... Behold, the virgin shall be with child and shall bear a son, and they shall call his name Immanuel..." (Matthew 1:21-23)	"behold, the virgin shall conceive and bear a Son, and you shall call His name Immanuel." (Isaiah 7:14, Orthodox Study Bible)	The Virgin Birth	"behold, the young woman is with child, and she shall bear a son, and she shall call his name Immanuel." (Isaiah 7:14, Complete Jewish Bible)
"And again, when he bringeth in the firstbegotten into the world, he saith, And let all the angels of God worship him." (Hebrews 1:6)	"Rejoice, ye heavens, with him, and let all the angels of God worship him" (Deuteronomy 32:43, Brenton's LXX)	The Deity of Christ	The MT of Deuteronomy 32:43 says nothing about angels worshiping the Messiah. (KJV, Jewish Bible, etc.)
Jesus said He fulfilled the OT prophecy to "proclaim liberty to the captives and recovery of sight to the blind" (Luke 4:18)	The OT prophecied that Messiah would "preach liberty to the captives and recovery of sight to the blind" (Isaiah 61:1, Orthodox Study Bible)	Jesus Healing the Blind	The MT of Isaiah 61:1 says nothing about the blind having their sight restored. (KJV, Jewish Bible, etc.)
Numerous NT passages mention Christ's hands and feet being pierced by crucifixion.	"They pierced my hands and my feet" (Psalm 21:17, Orthodox Study Bible)	The Crucifixion	"like a lion, my hands and my feet" (Psalm 22:17, Complete Jewish Bible)
"and in his name shall the Gentiles trust." (Matt. 12:21)	"and in his name shall the Gentiles trust." (Isaiah 42:4, Brenton's LXX)	Gentiles Trusting in Jesus' Name	"and the isles shall wait for his law." (Isaiah 42:4, KJV)

These are not random, inconsequential differences between the texts. Rather, these appear to be places where the Masoretes (or their forebears) had a varied selection of texts to consider, and their decisions were influenced by anti-Christian bias. Simply by choosing one Hebrew text over another, they were able to subvert the Incarnation, the virgin birth, the deity of Christ, His healing of the blind, His crucifixion, and His salvation of the Gentiles. The Jewish scribes were able to edit Jesus out of many important passages, simply by rejecting one Hebrew text, and selecting (or editing) another text instead.

Thus, the Masoretic Text has *not* perfectly preserved the original Hebrew text of Scripture. The Masoretes received corrupted texts to begin with, they used an alphabet which was radically different from the original Hebrew, they added countless vowel points which did not exist in the original, they excluded several books from the Old Testament scriptures, and they included a number of significant changes to prophecy and doctrine.

It would seem that the Septuagint (LXX) translation is not only far more *ancient* than the Masoretic Text; the Septuagint is far more *accurate* as well. It is a more faithful representation of the original Hebrew Scriptures.

Perhaps that is the reason why Jesus and the apostles frequently quoted from the Septuagint, and accorded it full authority as the inspired Word of God.

Which Bible is Better?

We have compared three popular English translations of the Bible: the King James Version (KJV), the New International Version (NIV), and the Orthodox Study Bible (OSB). In summary, we have found the following:

KJV & NIV	Orthodox Study Bible
• The apostle Paul misquotes Psalm 14, Psalm 4, and Isaiah 10.	• The apostle Paul correctly quotes Psalm 14, Psalm 4, and Isaiah 10.
• St. Stephen refers to Genesis 46 incorrectly.	• St. Stephen remembers Genesis 46 correctly.
• The apostle Peter misquotes Isaiah 53.	• The apostle Peter correctly quotes Isaiah 53.
• Jesus misreads Isaiah 61	• Jesus reads Isaiah 61 correctly.
• We are not told who Job was.	• Job was the King of Edom, he was Esau's grandson, and he will participate in the resurrection of the dead.
• The book of Esther contains no prophecy, no prayer, and no mention of God.	• The book of Esther contains divine prophecy, exemplary prayers, and numerous instances where God is honored and praised.
• Hebrews 11 references the Maccabean martyrs, yet their story is missing.	• Hebrews 11 references the Maccabean martyrs, and their story is in the Old Testament book of 1 Maccabees.
• The book of Matthew contains fulfillment to a prophecy in the book of Wisdom. But the book of Wisdom has been removed from both the KJV and the NIV.	• The book of Wisdom contains an impressive prophecy of Christ, the Son of God. The prophecy is fulfilled in the book of Matthew.
• Much of the KJV and NIV was translated from the Masoretic Text.	• Much of the OSB was translated from the Septuagint.

There are many other side-by-side comparisons that could be made, but this list will suffice for our present study. In this brief overview, we have seen that there are many important differences from one version of the Bible to another. Different Bibles have different numbers of books. An individual book can vary from one Bible to another. Each Bible may have a slightly different copy of the book of Psalms, or the book of Isaiah, for instance.

The differences between the Septuagint and the Masoretic Text can account for many of the differences that are found between Protestant versions of the Bible, such as the KJV and NIV, and Orthodox versions of the Bible, such as the OSB.

Which version of the Bible is right for you? Well, that depends . . .

Which Bible do you believe most accurately preserves God's Word?

Christ the King
Orthodox Church
679 2nd St.
Omaha, IL 62871

www.omahaorthodox.com

Christ the King
Orthodox Church
679 2nd St.
Omaha, IL 62871

www.omahaorthodox.com